Given to _____

On this _____ day of _____

By _____

With this special message . . .

_____

_____

Bible Promises

Itty Bitty™ Books

PRECIOUS MOMENTS™

Bible Promises

SAM BUTCHER

THOMAS NELSON PUBLISHERS
Nashville

ITTY BITTY™ BOOKS

Published in Nashville, Tennessee, by Thomas Nelson,
Inc., and distributed in Canada by Lawson Falle, Ltd.,
Cambridge, Ontario.

Library of Congress
Cataloging-in-Publication Data

Butcher, Samuel J. (Samuel John), 1939–
  Precious Moments Bible promises / Sam Butcher
     p.   cm. — (Itty bitty)
  Summary: A collection of verses from the King
James and Good News Bibles, arranged under the
headings "Promises of Blessings," "Promises for
Personal Needs," and "Promises for Relationships."
  ISBN 0-8407-4263-0 (TR) ISBN 0-8407-6768-4 (MM)
  1. Bible—Picture Bibles. 2. Promises—Religious
aspects—Christianity—Juvenile literature.
[1. Bible—Selections.]
I. Butcher, Samuel J. (Samuel John), 1939–
II. Title. III. Title: Bible promises. IV. Series.
BS560 1992
220.5´2036—dc20   92–3666
                       CIP
                       AC

Printed in Hong Kong.

Contents

Introduction

Even the most casual collector of Precious Moments™ figurines senses the connection between the names of the figurines and verses in the Bible. This is no coincidence. Sam Butcher's faith has inspired the creation of the Precious Moments™ illustrations.

Through the years Sam met many people who had problems in their lives and needed someone to tell them, "I'm here if you need me." Sam never liked to push people. So, instead, he made individual greeting cards. He found people really responded and would say, "If you would do greeting cards like these, so many people would be blessed."

This book is the first time Sam has shared the complete Bible verses that inspired the Precious Moments™ art and figurines. He has divided the book into three sections: Promises of Blessings, Promises for Personal Needs, and Promises for Relationships. He shares these passages of Scripture with you so that you might be able to read them at times when you are having difficulty or needing an insight into your everyday life.

Promises of
Blessings

Blessed Are the Peacemakers

Matthew 5:9: "Blessed are the peacemakers."

Blessed are the peacemakers,
For they shall be called sons of God.

Blessed are those who
are persecuted for
righteousness' sake,
For theirs is the
kingdom of
heaven. . . .

"Rejoice and be exceedingly glad, for great is your reward in heaven, for so they persecuted the prophets who were before you."

Matthew 5:9–10, 12

Make a Joyful Noise

Psalm 100:1: "Make a joyful shout to the Lord."

Make a joyful shout to the Lord, all you lands!
Serve the Lord with gladness;
Come before His presence with singing.

Know that the Lord, He
   is God;
It is He who has made
   us, and not we
   ourselves;
We are His people and
   the sheep of His
   pasture.

Enter into His gates
    with thanksgiving.
And into His courts
    with praise.
Be thankful to Him,
    and bless His name.
For the Lord is good;
His mercy is
    everlasting,
And His truth endures
    to all generations.

Psalm 100

To God
Be the Glory

*Psalm 29:2: "Praise the
Lord's glorious name,"*

Praise the Lord, you
heavenly beings;
praise His glory and
power.

Praise the Lord's glorious name; bow down before the Holy One when He appears. . . .

23

The Lord gives strength
to His people and
blesses them with
peace.

Psalm 29:1-2, 11

Promises for
Personal Needs

The Lord Is My Shepherd

Psalm 23:1: "The Lord is my shepherd."

The Lord is my
   shepherd;
I shall not want.

He makes me to lie
   down in green
   pastures;
He leads me beside the
   still waters.
He restores my soul;
He leads me in the
   paths of righteousness
For His name's sake.

Yea, though I walk
through the valley of
the shadow of death,
I will fear no evil;
For You are with me;
Your rod and Your staff,
they comfort me.

You prepare a table
   before me in the
   presence of my
   enemies;
You anoint my head
   with oil;
My cup runs over.

Surely goodness and
  mercy shall follow me
All the days of my life;
And I will dwell in the
  house of the Lord
Forever.

Psalm 23

His Burden Is Light

Matthew 11:30: "For My yoke is easy and My burden is light."

"Come to Me, all you who labor and are heavy laden, and I will give you rest.

"Take My yoke upon you and learn from Me, for I am gentle and lowly in heart, and you will find rest for your souls.

"For My yoke is easy
and *My burden is light."*
Matthew 11:28–30

If God Be for Us, Who Can Be Against Us?

Romans 8:31: "If God is for us, who can be against us?"

In view of all this, what can we say? If God is for us, who can be against us? . . .

Who, then, can separate
   us from the love of
   Christ?
Can trouble do it?

Or hardship or
  persecution or hunger
  or poverty or danger
  or death?

For I am certain that
nothing can separate
us from His love:

Neither the present nor
the future,
Neither the world above
nor the world below.

Romans 8:31, 35, 38

Trust in the Lord

Psalm 37:3: "Trust in the Lord."

Trust in the Lord and do good;
Live in the land and be safe.
Seek your happiness in the Lord.
And He will give you your heart's desire.

Give yourself to the
Lord.
Trust in Him, and He
will help you.
He will make your
righteousness shine
like the noonday
sun . . .

Soon the wicked will
   disappear;
You may look for them,
   but you won't find
   them.
But the humble will
   possess the land
And enjoy prosperity
   and peace.
   Psalm 37:3–6, 10–12

Jesus Is the Light

John 8:12: "I am the light of the world."

Jesus spoke to the Pharisees again. *"I am the light of the world,"* He said. "Whoever follows Me will have the light of life and will never walk in darkness."

John 8:12

Onward Christian Soldiers

Ephesians 6:11: "Put on all the armor that God gives you."

Put on all the armor
  that God gives you,
So that you will be able
  to stand up against
  the Devil's evil
  tricks. . . .

So stand ready,
With truth as a belt
   tight around your
   waist,
With righteousness as
   your breastplate,
And as your shoes the
   readiness to announce
   the Good News of
   peace.

At all times carry faith
  as a shield.
For with it you will be
  able to put out all the
  burning arrows shot
  by the Evil One.

And accept salvation as
   a helmet.
And the word of God as
   the sword which the
   Spirit gives you.

Do all this in prayer,
asking for God's help.
Ephesians 6:11, 14–18

No Tears
Past the Gate

I praise you, Lord,
   because you have
   saved me and kept
   my enemies from
   gloating over me.

I cried to you for help, O Lord my God, and you healed me; you kept me from the grave.

I was on my way to the
depths below, but you
restored my life.
Sing praise to the Lord,
all his faithful people!

Remember what the
Holy One has done,
and give him thanks!
His anger lasts only a
moment, his goodness
for a lifetime.

Tears may flow in the
   night, but joy comes
   in the morning. . . .
Lord, you are my God; I
   will give you thanks
   forever.

Psalm 30:1–5; 11, 12

Promises for
Relationships

Love Is Kind

1 Corinthians 13:4: "Love suffers long and is kind."

Though I speak with the tongues of men and of angels but have not love, I have become as sounding brass or a clanging cymbal.

And though I have a
gift of prophecy, and
understand all
mysteries and all
knowledge, and though
I have all faith, so that
I could remove
mountains, but have not
love, I am nothing. . . .

Love suffers long and is kind; love does not envy; love does not parade itself, is not puffed up.

1 Corinthians 13:1–4

Love Beareth All Things

1 Corinthians 13:7 "Love bears all things."

Love does not behave rudely, does not seek its own, is not provoked, thinks no evil;

Does not rejoice in
iniquity, but rejoices in
the truth;

Love bears all things,
believes all things,
hopes all things,
endures all things.
1 Corinthians 13:5–7

Love One Another

John 15:12: "Love one another."

"My commandment is this: *love one another,* just as I love you.

"And you are My friends if you do what I command you. . . .

"You did not choose Me; I chose you and appointed you to go and bear much fruit, the kind of fruit that endures. And so the Father will give you whatever you ask of Him in My name.

"This, then, is what I command you: *love one another.*"

   John 15:12–14, 16–17

Bear One Another's Burdens

Galatians 6:2: "Help carry one another's burdens."

My brothers, if someone
is caught in any kind of
wrongdoing, those of
you who are spiritual
should set him right;
but you must do it in a
gentle way. . . .

Help carry one another's burdens, and in this way you will obey the law of Christ.

Galatians 6:1, 2

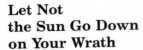

Let Not the Sun Go Down on Your Wrath

Ephesians 4:26: "Do not let the sun go down on your wrath."

This I say, therefore, and testify in the Lord, that you should no longer walk as the rest of the Gentiles walk. . . .

Therefore, putting away lying, each one speak truth with his neighbor, for we are members of one another.

"Be angry, and do not sin": *do not let the sun go down on your wrath,* nor give place to the devil.

Ephesians 4:17, 25–27

God Loves a Cheerful Giver

2 Corinthians 9:7: "For God loves a cheerful giver."

But this I say: He who sows sparingly will also reap sparingly, and he who sows bountifully will also reap bountifully.

So let each one give as he purposed in his heart, not grudgingly or of necessity; *for God loves a cheerful giver.*

2 Corinthians 9:6–7

Love Never Fails

1 Corinthians 13:8 "Love never fails."

Love never fails. But whether there are prophecies, they will fail; whether there are tongues, they will cease; whether there is knowledge, it will vanish away.

For we know in part
and we prophesy in
part.

But when that which is
perfect has come, then
that which is in part
will be done away. . . .

And now abide faith,
hope, love, these three;
but the greatest of these
is love.

1 Corinthians 13:8–10, 13